Kids' Gratitude

Kids' Gratitude

Thank you, oh World

David OLUBIYI

Dabim Support Services Inc.

To all the curious hearts, the kind souls, and the grateful spirits who find wonder, beauty, and grace in every corner of our magnificent world. Your appreciation, your gratitude, and your love for this wondrous planet are the true sources of inspiration for this book. May it serve as a reminder of the blessings that surround us, and may it inspire us all to say, "Thank you, oh world," with hearts full of love and gratitude.

Thank you, oh world, for colors so bright,

For sunny days and stars in the night.

For fluffy clouds that float up high,

And birds that sing as they pass by.

Thank you, dear rain, for watering the land,
For filling rivers and making trees grand.
For splashing puddles and making flowers grow,
For cleansing the earth with your gentle flow.

Thank you, dear moon, for lighting up the night,

For casting your glow with a gentle might.

For guiding lost souls and calming our fears,

For whispering secrets in our dreaming ears.

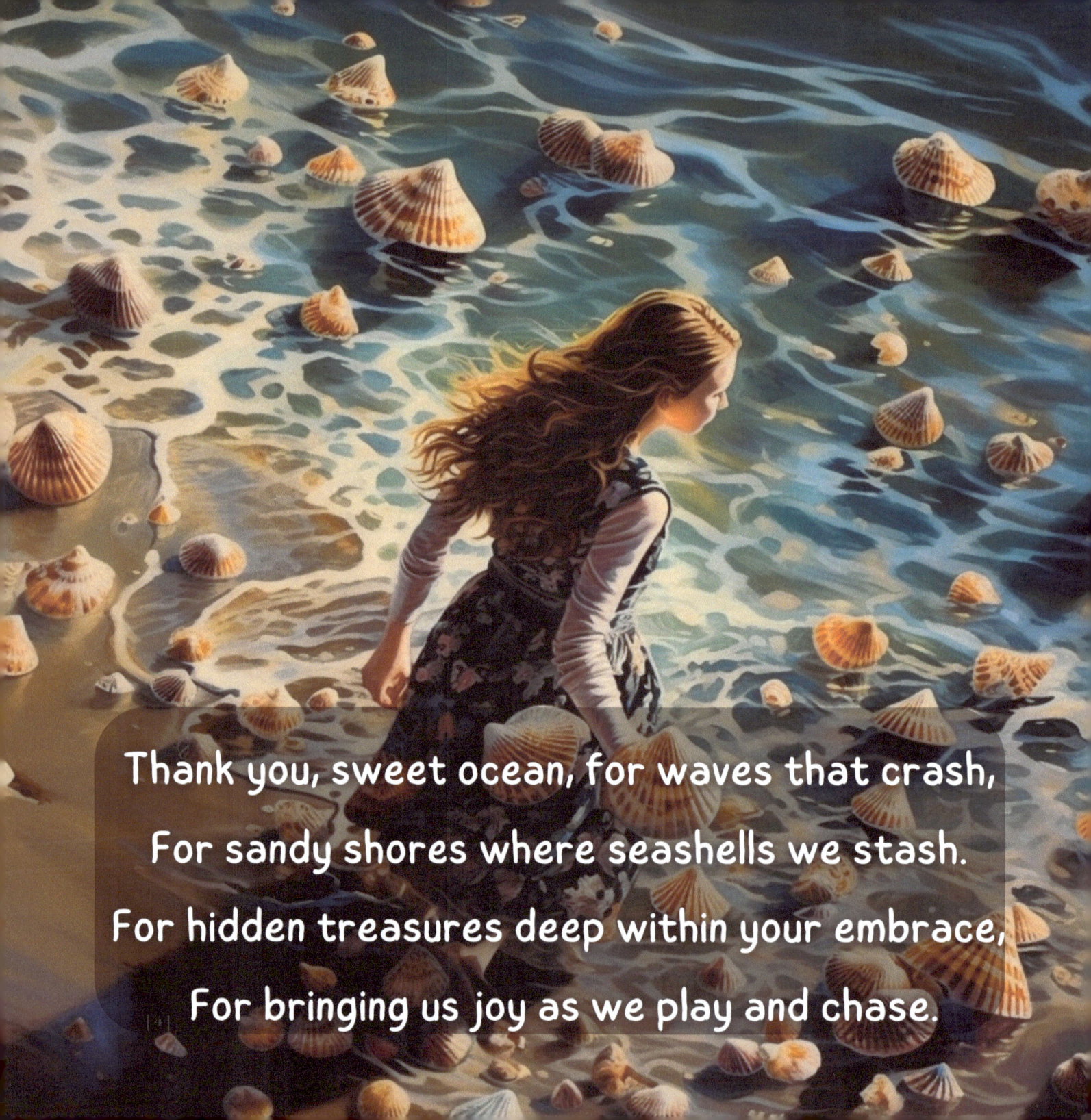

Thank you, sweet ocean, for waves that crash,
For sandy shores where seashells we stash.
For hidden treasures deep within your embrace,
For bringing us joy as we play and chase.

Thank you, dear wind, for a playful breeze, For rustling leaves on the tall, swaying trees. For lifting kites up high in the sky, For carrying whispers as they pass by.

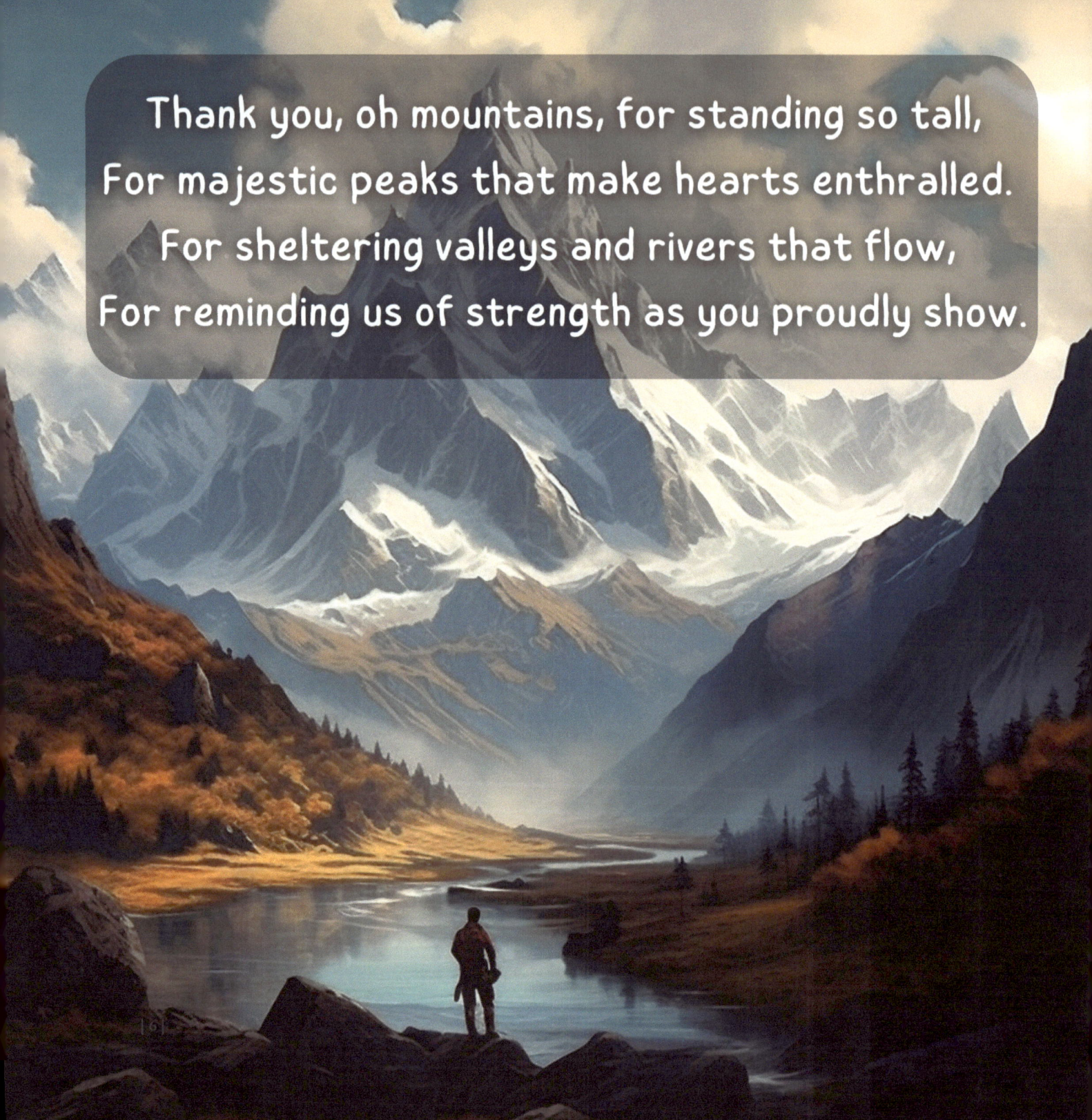

Thank you, oh mountains, for standing so tall,
For majestic peaks that make hearts enthralled.
For sheltering valleys and rivers that flow,
For reminding us of strength as you proudly show.

Thank you, dear friends, for laughter and fun,
For sharing adventures, one by one.
For being there through thick and thin,
For showing us love and the warmth within.

Thank you, kind teachers, for knowledge you share,
For guiding us gently with love and care.
For nurturing minds and igniting a spark,
For helping us grow and make our mark.

Thank you, dear parents, for love so deep,

For the sleepless nights when we couldn't sleep.

For comforting hugs and words that inspire,

For shaping us with love that never tires.

Thank you, dear pets, for your loyal hearts,

For cuddles and kisses, the cutest of arts.

For teaching us patience and unconditional love,

For being a blessing sent from above.

Thank you, dear books, for stories untold,
For taking us on adventures, bold and bold.
For expanding our minds and imagination's flight,
For opening doors to worlds of pure delight.

Thank you, oh sun, for warmth on our skin, For brightening days with your radiant grin. For painting the sky with your golden hue, For reminding us that each day is new.

Thank you, sweet music, for melodies so grand,
For lifting our spirits with your magical band.
For soothing our souls when we're feeling down,
For filling our hearts with a harmonious sound.

Thank you, dear flowers, for fragrant delight,
For blooming in gardens, a mesmerizing sight.
For painting the world with colors so bright,
For spreading joy with your petals in flight.

Thank you, dear food, for nourishing our souls,

For filling our bellies and making us whole.

For flavors and spices that dance on our tongues,

For the pleasure of eating and the joy it brings.

Thank you, dear rainbows, for your vibrant arc,

For filling the sky with a colorful spark.

For reminding us of beauty after the storm,

For promising hope in each vibrant form.

Thank you, dear stars, for twinkling above, For filling
the night sky with a celestial love.
For granting wishes with your mystical might,
For guiding us through the darkness with light.

Thank you, dear world, for all that you give,

For teaching us how to truly live.

For every moment, big or small,

Thank you, thank you, one and all.

18

Thank you, dear playground, for laughter and play,

For swings and slides to brighten our day.

For climbing structures and sand-filled pits,

For endless adventures and childhood bliss.

Thank you, dear seasons, for your ever-changing ways,

For bringing us joy with each passing phase.

For blooming flowers in spring's gentle embrace,

For warm summer days and leaves in fall's grace.

Thank you, dear dreams, for taking us far,
For imagination's journey, like a shooting star.
For the magic and wonder you bring in the night,
For inspiring us to reach for new heights.

Thank you, dear kindness, for spreading like wildfire,

For acts of compassion that never tire.

For lending a hand to those in need,

For sowing seeds of love through every good deed.

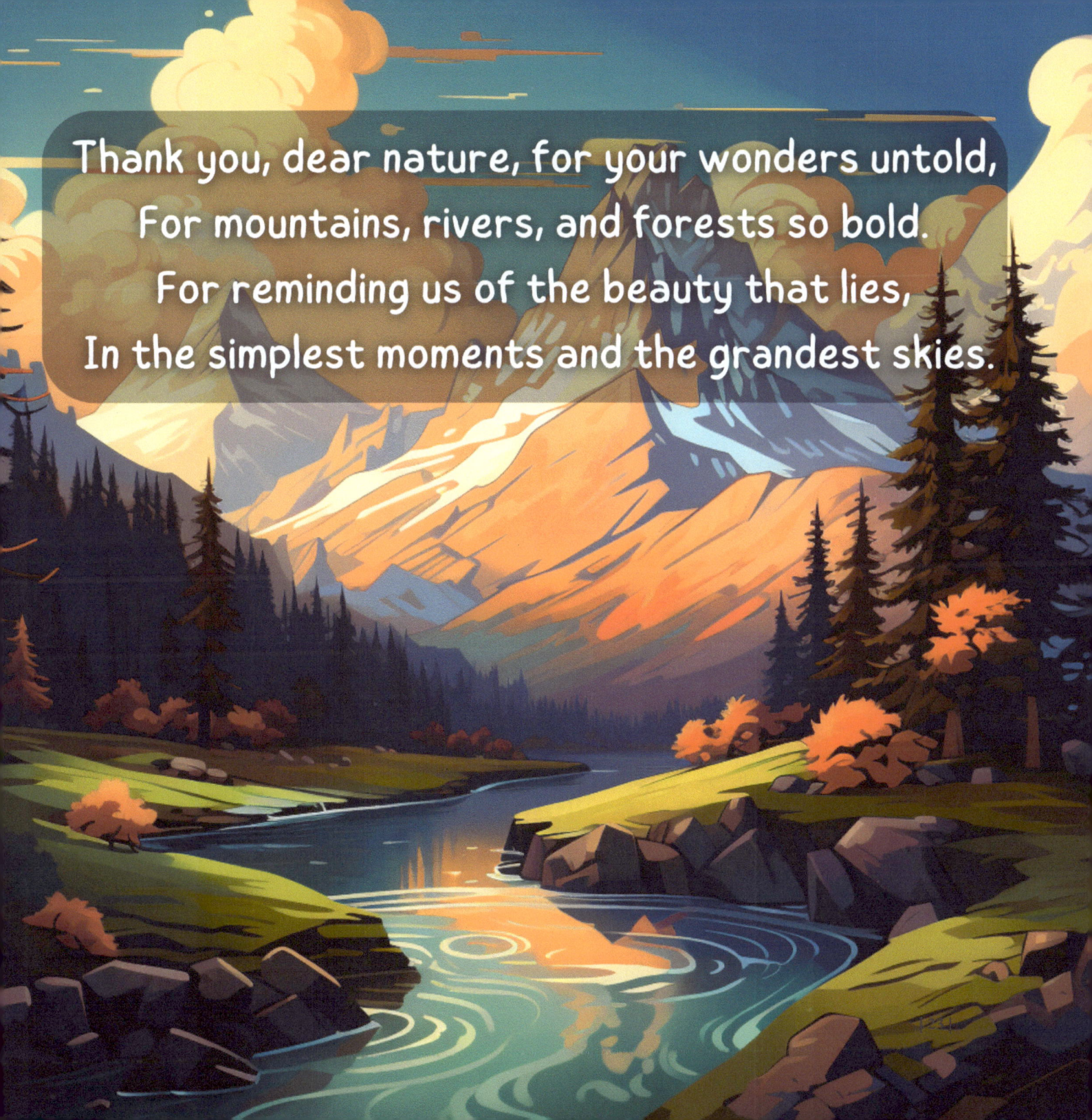

Thank you, dear nature, for your wonders untold,
For mountains, rivers, and forests so bold.
For reminding us of the beauty that lies,
In the simplest moments and the grandest skies.

Thank you, dear forgiveness, for healing our pain,
For freeing our hearts from the burden and strain.
For letting go of grudges and finding release,
For granting us peace and inner calmness increase.

Thank you, dear hope, for shining so bright,
For illuminating the darkest of night.
For inspiring us to believe in a better tomorrow,
For fueling our spirits with strength to borrow.

Thank you, dear sunsets, for painting the sky,

For a breathtaking beauty that makes us sigh.

For hues of orange, pink, and gold,

For moments of tranquility that never get old.

Thank you, dear curiosity, for sparking our minds,
For encouraging exploration of various kinds.
For the thirst for knowledge and the joy it brings,
For widening our horizons and giving us wings.

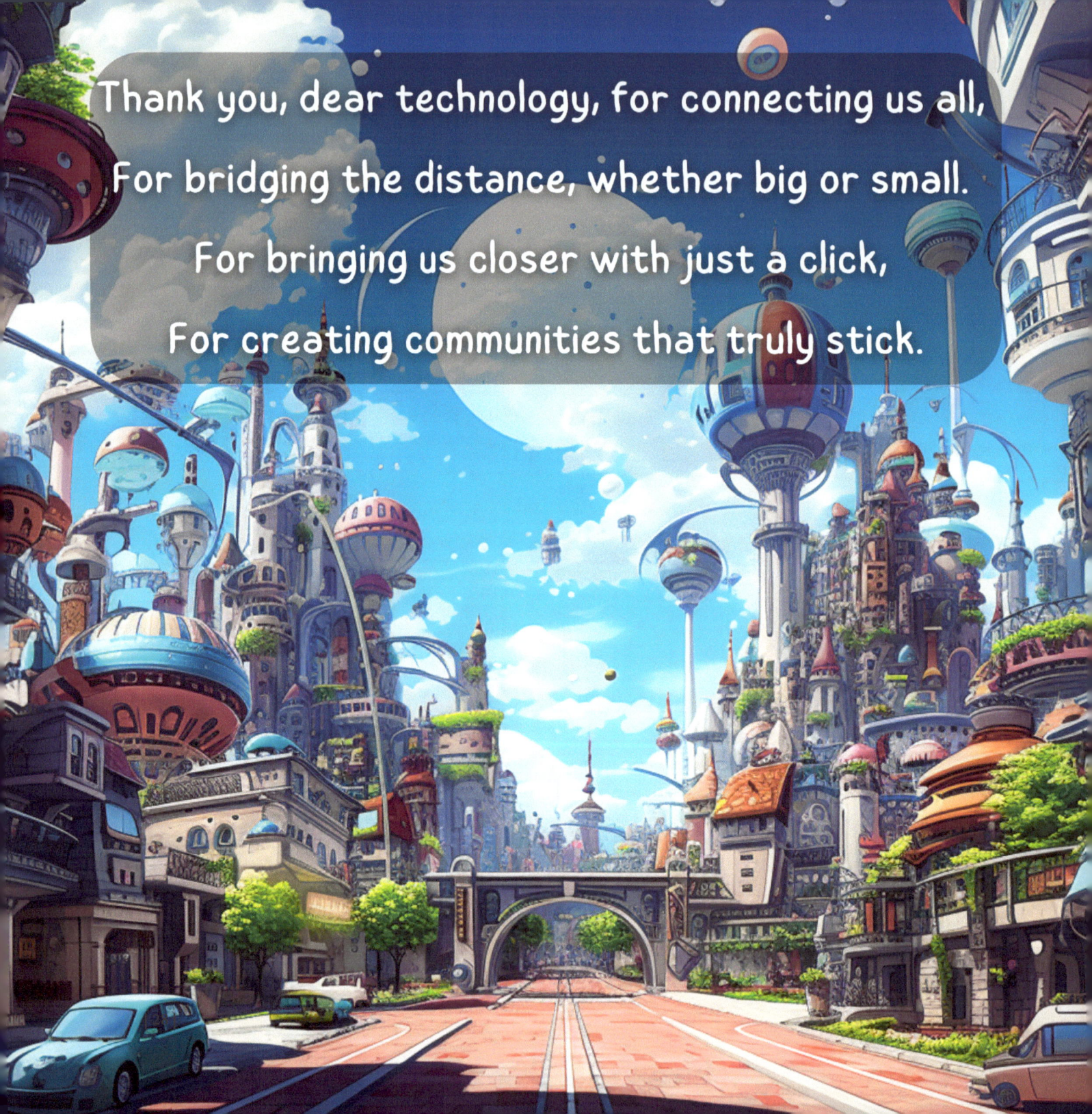

Thank you, dear technology, for connecting us all,
For bridging the distance, whether big or small.
For bringing us closer with just a click,
For creating communities that truly stick.

Thank you, dear sunrise, for a brand-new day,

For a fresh start and opportunities that lay.

For painting the horizon with a golden hue,

For inspiring us to begin anew.

Thank you, dear celebration, for joyful times,
For marking milestones with laughter and rhymes.
For gathering loved ones, creating cherished memories,
For strengthening bonds and weaving life's stories.

Thank you, dear love, for connecting us all,
For the bonds that hold us, standing tall.
For the warmth in our hearts, so pure and true,
For reminding us of the beauty in me and you.

Thank you, dear health, for keeping us strong,
For the gift of wellness that lasts long.
For allowing us to live life to the fullest,
For granting us energy and vitality, the purest.

Thank you, dear world,
for all that you provide,
For the wonders and
beauty that cannot be
denied.
For the interconnectedness
we all share,
For reminding us
to live with love and care.

David Olubiyi is a passionate writer and explorer of the human spirit, known for weaving tales that celebrate the beauty of life and the wonders of the world. With a heart brimming with gratitude and a keen eye for the extraordinary in the ordinary, David Olubiyi has crafted "Thank You, Oh World" as a testament to the boundless blessings that our planet bestows upon us.

"Thank You, Oh World" is David's heartfelt ode to the planet that has offered us boundless gifts, and a reminder to pause, reflect, and give thanks for the wonders that surround us every day. Through their writing, David hopes to inspire readers to embrace the beauty of our world with open hearts and grateful spirits, and to carry the message of gratitude into their own lives.

David Olubiyi resides in Canada, where he continue to write, explore, and find inspiration in the world's endless marvels.

www.ingramcontent.com/pod-product-compliance
Lightning Source LLC
Chambersburg PA
CBHW041556120626
46551CB00002B/226